BASIC STATEMENTS and
Health Treatment of Truth.

A SYSTEM OF INSTRUCTION in
Divine Science Treatment for Class Training,
and FOR
HOME AND PRIVATE USE.

Perceived Through a Study of Divine Science, and Through Repeated Demonstration Proven to be Impersonal and Applicable Alike to All.

By
Malinda E. CRAMER,
Author of "Lessons in Science and Healing."
Editor of "Harmony."

San Francisco, 1893.

Basic Statements and

Health Treatment of Truth

By Malinda E. Cramer

© WiseWoman Press 2015
Managing Editor: Michael Terranova

ISBN: 978-0945385-88-2

WiseWoman Press
Vancouver, WA 98665

www.wisewomanpress.com
www.emmacurtishopkins.com

MALINDA E. CRAMER.

Publisher's note

Wise Woman Press publishes all of Emma Curtis Hopkins' works. The reason for publishing a work by Malinda Cramer is to introduce Ms. Cramer to the followers of Emma's teachings.

It is also important to make it known that Malinda Cramer was not a student of Emma as quoted in many books and on the internet. After reading Malinda Cramer's books it becomes clear she had made her own connection with Spirit and had created a teaching style and a school to teach it in. They were contemporaries and did meet and support each other.

Both Malinda and Emma found their avenues to Spirit by their own healings, and were able to create ways to teach it to others.

It is a joy to make sure these materials are kept in print and available to future generations.

Rev. Michael Terranova
Wise Woman Press

M. E. Cramer

INTRODUCTION
By Nina Russell

"America shall introduce a pure religion."
~Ralph Waldo Emerson

What is a pure religion? It is not the human theories or beliefs that humankind has been using for centuries without making great headway spiritually. A pure religion is one that comes from spiritual enlightenment and the one who becomes spiritually enlightened passes this understanding on to those who are ready and desiring to learn.

Spiritual enlightenment came to Malinda Cramer one early morning in 1885 when she appealed to the Divine with the question "Is there any way out of these conditions; is there any Power in the vast Universe that can heal me?" Malinda had been under medical treatment for 23 out of 25 years of invalidism with no significant improvement. Having had all the medical treatments available to her at the time, she was tired of the medical merry-go-around, and now was refusing more useless treatments.

Immediately after asking the question to the Divine, she had an experience that forever changed not only her life, but the lives of many people in future generations. She realized the omnipresence of God which was more real than any material object in front of her. Suddenly she understood and experienced all that had been taught to her about God. She felt one with this Holy Presence and knew it to be her life. She also realized and experienced that all are in the embrace of one eternal God, Good. She experienced Light describing it as a "Consuming fire." As she looked out over the world, she had the realization of the Biblical verse "a New heaven and a new earth, old things had passed away." What passed away was the illness. Now what is taught is "A Truth once understood in consciousness, demonstrates itself." Her consciousness became filled with God's Truth, so naturally there was a change in the outer or the physical person. Not long afterwards, her friends, seeing the miraculous change in her, asked her for prayer treatments so they might be well also.

There are always the doubters – the ones who say that her experience was a delusion. But others have had these miraculous experiences: the Catholics have produced mystics, those who have had an experience of God. Saint Hildegard of Bingen was one of those. Born in 1098, she became a nun, and when she was 42 years old, she had an experience similar to Malinda Cramer's. She experienced Light, and suddenly she truly understood spiritually all she had been taught. Saint Hildegard accomplished much after the experience, including taking bishops, popes and emperors to task, which was not easy for a woman in a male dominated age. She also brought together art, science and religion. The enlightenment experience is a universal experience, not limited to a specific religion or denomination.

Ralph Waldo Emerson explains this experience: "The soul's communication of truth is the highest event in nature, since it then does not give somewhat from itself, but gives itself, or passes into and becomes that man whom it enlightens; or in proportion to that truth he receives, it takes him to itself. . . . . . This communication is an influx of the Divine mind into our mind."

After two years of doing healing prayer treatments for people, Malinda Cramer began teaching. There are people looking for spiritual teachers, but the quality of the teachers varies greatly. If one wants to have his child take piano lessons, does he not select the best one so the child will develop good habits instead of getting a lesser teacher, learning bad habits, then having to re-learn? Cramer's teachings were probably the highest available in that part of the country. We now have the original teachings available to us in this age, even though it may be in the language of the 1800s. This is a small issue that is overcome by self-discipline, deciding to persevere in order to grow spiritually.

Cramer's teachings are not based on limited human opinion, but on spiritual revelation. The writings in this book are based on Truth, the absolute Truth of God, not the relative truth of humankind. Man's idea of truth is constantly changing; God's Truth is eternal, never changing. Therefore, understanding the teachings in this book has the potential to change one's life if they are understood spiritually, not just on the mental level. As one's spiritual consciousness grows and expands, one's life also changes. Consciousness is cause, and our outer life is effect. Change consciousness and the effect, the outer life, changes in proportion. How is this to be accomplished? By studying, contemplating, praying, meditating and applying Truth, one can speed one's spiritual growth. This is why we are on Earth, living only a certain number of years, then going on - we are here to grow spiritually!

"But seek ye first the kingdom of God, and his righteousness (right or spiritual thinking); and all these things shall be added unto you." (Matthew 6:33) This is a great Truth that many have not recognized. It is finding the kingdom of God – the teachings which bring us to a higher consciousness (cause), and the outer things needed for life are added (effect). In these teachings, you will find much spiritual growth. Another way that Jesus put this Truth is "And ye shall know the truth, and the truth shall make you free." (John 8:32) This statement is open ended – Truth can free one physically, mentally, morally and financially. The Truth of God is always freedom – never bondage to any human or earthly limitation. But the Truth must be understood spiritually which is Cramer's goal – to help others toward greater spiritual understanding.

M. E. Cramer

Malinda Cramer was a blessing to the many people who had the advantage to learn from her enlightenment, her spiritual revelations. But do not accept what she says at face or surface value. Contemplate and meditate on the teachings to help bring out their full meaning. Your spiritual growth can be great as you do this. May you be blessed by the reading and application of Cramer's teachings!

PREFACE.

The arrangement of this consecutive course of condensed lessons under the heading of BASIC STATEMENTS and Treatment, is designed to be a simple, practical method which, when understood and practiced, will enable students to realize within themselves and for others, wholeness; which is pure Being, perfect thought and the result of such thought. Wholeness means health, satisfaction and success in general.

Wholeness, includes the all of Life, Intelligence, Truth and Substance, for which all are seeking.

M. E. Cramer

DIVINE SCIENCE STATEMENTS and HEALTH TREATMENT.

CONTENTS.

M. E. Cramer

DIVINE SCIENCE STATEMENTS

AND

HEALTH TREATMENT.

PART I.

HEALING BY THE CHRIST METHOD.

The basis of the manifestation of power in the Christ Method of Healing is a realized knowledge of the at-one-ment of man with God. "I and my Father are one" means one and the same, and not two. The Creator of an ever-present, living creation must necessarily be an infinite and limitless Creator, from eternity to eternity, whence, there is no finite being to be limited, and no limitation.

Most people believe that creation was an event of the past, and that creative action ceased with the accomplishment of that event. Where this is believed, creation is claimed to belong unto time and place. This view is a false conception, for whatever lives, lives within, and unto the omnipresent God, or Creator, and

1

is, therefore, living within and unto eternity; hence, must have being, beginning, finishing, and ending in God, now and in the eternal *now*. If the being and beginning of all that exists was not in eternity, existence would have no relationship with God now. "The way, the truth, and the life," must be the origin and the beginning of all living things; hence, all things must find an ending where they begin. As *I* Am the Word which is the light of the world, and of every man that cometh into the world, everything that lives within Me is illumined with My glory, even as the burning bush was to Moses, aflame with the light of My Holy presence.

Not until we conceive that now are all things living unto eternity, and not unto time, are we able to witness the beginning of creation. When we cease thinking, speaking, and acting, as if the body, or anything possessed by us, belongs unto time, and is dependent on place, we shall have ceased talking about death, and planning for the grave. A full understanding of the living truth of what we are is Divine Science, or Knowledge of God in creation; for creation is Self-manifestation.

HEALING

The attention of the people is, in various ways, being called to the Christ Method of Healing. Some are interested through hearing of others having been healed, and are thus caused to give it their consideration; wanting healing, as they do, either for themselves or others, they are induced to try this method, which results in the health and satisfaction for which they have long sought.

They who say, "If one can be healed, another can; hence, healing is for me," speak wisely. They virtually declare the eternal truth for themselves, that "God is no respect of persons." This, and similar decisions, make receptive all mental conditions and beliefs, and is a preparation for successful results. Again, others are advised by friends to try the Christ Method; and as they have done all they knew to be done-having exhausted every method that has been thought out for the salvation of man-they accept the advice, and resolve to try again, and are made whole.

The methods by which people are induced to investigate Science and Truth's practice may vary, but

3

what all are seeking to know is, when and how to begin. *Now* is always the accepted time. The moment you want to be healed is the right time to commence the work. It is understood by all that there can be no result without a beginning, and no beginning but action, and no action without result following. Hence, the beginning must necessarily precede the result. There is something for you to do, though the nature of the work to be done differs from every previous attempt made to regain your health. Much has been said in the class-room, and written, explanatory of methods by which healing is done, which are considered helpful in their nature; but in the Christ method a knowledge of true Being, and of being that which is whole, is the one consideration.

How can we heal others when there is a beam in our own eye? A belief that there is something in truth, or that has reality, the obverse of God, will see motes and blemishes in others; and that which describes false belief as real, is false belief itself. No one believes error to be truth, who knows what truth is. When a child understands the principle by which to solve his problem, he does not believe that error is truth, or that a mistake stands for true calculation.

The responsibility as to the result of Treatment does not rest exclusively with the person employed in giving the treatment. Christ, in the patient, who is "the Way, the Truth, and the Life," compels no one to accept Him, and be whole in his thought and belief, God creates all things, but does not create beliefs concerning them. It is a matter of free will whether we pronounce with Him, or otherwise. "Choose ye this day whom ye will serve," whether it be the truth that the infinite whole is God, and is perfect, or whether it be the false supposition that there is something else that is imperfect, which is not Truth. Those wanting to be healed must do their part and be willing to recognize and receive unto themselves, and be that which is whole. The record of Life says that we have eternal life with God. This being true, we must necessarily have eternal health, and be satisfied and happy.

The teaching of Jesus stands above all other, in that he taught that a knowledge of the Truth, when applied, healed, or put an end to all sickness; for there can be no sickness in God or Good, hence can be none in Truth. His practice was proof of the truth of his preaching; for he not only healed the sick when called upon to do so, but the command to the disciples was to go forth into all the world, and preach the gospel unto every creature under heaven, and heal the sick. It is not sufficient unto Truth to think the thought of truth for a portion of the earth; but it must erase the false belief of the world's apostasy from God; we must proceed forth from the Holy Spirit into all the world, even unto the ends of the earth.

"Go show yourselves to the Priests," Jesus said unto the ten lepers who called upon him to have mercy on them. The appeal was made as he approached, which, spiritually speaking, made the conjunction or at-one-ment in thought, and they went their way; but their way was according to his direction or commandment, and the result was a realization of wholeness; they were cleansed.

The first requirement in the Christ method of healing is that of giving up the false supposition and selfish belief of a self-hood separate from God. This change of thought is the spiritual act of baptizing unto repentance, which must precede the taking on of at-one-ment, which is baptism of the Holy Spirit. At-one-ment is the yoke that is easy, or it is the bond of union which makes light all burdens.

Where two are agreed upon earth as touching any one thing there is at-one-ment, and I Am is in the midst. What is agreed upon shall be granted unto them. No line is to be drawn between the one employed in giving treatment and the one receiving. The two should agree; hence, be one concerning the Truth which is asked for. If it be health, which is the freedom and harmony of Truth that is sought to be realized, the first thing to do is to agree that health *is*, and is for you; and if for you, it is present; for what is not present cannot be realized, enjoyed, or demonstrated. In this you have the whole plan of success. You have now determined to shape your thought, word, and deed, according to the truth of what *is*, and is for you, and is at hand. So, there is no postponement, neither is there seeking for something to come from afar.

M. E. Cramer

"No" should never be taken for an answer, and in order to prove that "No" is not an accepted answer you are to cease making negative claims. God accepts no excuses, even as the principle in mathematics will accept no excuse in the solution of a problem, but demands that the principle be adhered to and demonstrated in the example. Make your claims according to Truth. Claim to be what *is* Truth, and your words will be words of Life - the pure, white "Yes" of God. The Canaanitish woman was so determined to have her daughter healed that she refused to recognize any obstacle to that result. All should be thus determined who ask for healing, and the result following will be one and the same.

As the word which was with God, and was God, made the world, and is its light and life, you should stop discussing the question as to whether it is God's will that you be healed, or made to realize wholeness. The will of an all-powerful God to make whole must be one and the same at all times. God must be without variation or shadow of turning. His will must be for the absolute perfection and goodness of each one, in every respect. Hence, the habit of setting up obstacles, claiming difficulties, and making excuses must be given up. The infinite All, when accepted as being all Good, or God, proves to be health, success, and harmony without limit. After having heard the Truth, nothing but a willingness to continue in old lines of thought and belief can hinder any one from having a full realization of wholeness. Since it is God's will that all should feel well, through right habit of thought, there is no reason why all should not enjoy health. It is an easy matter to reject the belief that there are difficulties to be overcome, and obstacles in the way, or excuses to be made; and to accept the whole Truth, and know true freedom. Begin your work at once by saying: What has been done, I can do. I can realize myself to be whole. Speak these words in faith, and persist in acting in line with them; actions speak louder than words, sometimes.

M. E. Cramer

BE SINCERE IN ALL EFFORT.

If it be true that you have sought in many ways and spent a fortune in your search for health, and have failed to find, do not hesitate to try the Christ method. It will heal you. Your past experience has embraced methods of treatment, accompanied with hope of getting well, which, at best, can only change one condition for another. These changes have been brought about by change of locality, of scenery, or perhaps by a few little pellets. These changes are made only in belief, and to condition, but do not touch the plane of eternal Life, or Being; hence, do not touch unchanging health. The Christ method of healing proves that wholeness alone is in Truth. It demonstrates that health is eternal with God; that success is ever at hand. Your past experience has been but a hope of getting well. Now, try the only true method of knowledge and faith---that of *being* well. "Be ye perfect, even as your Father in heaven is perfect." Perfect being must necessarily precede perfect thinking; and perfect thinking must precede perfect results, either in words, deeds, or sensations. This is infallible law.

If physicians have said that your case is incurable; if they have exhausted their skill upon you, and said there is no help for you, remember, their skill is in administering external remedies and in performing operations. "In vain shalt thou use many medicines, for thou shalt not be cured." Their skill is not that of bearing fruit of the spirit of Truth, and creating anew, which is the only true health there is; healing is producing results direct from Spirit, or Principle. Take no thought of what your friends have said about your case. Let your determination to succeed be a matter wholly between you and God. God never pronounces against any one, and will not say that your case is incurable or hopeless. He has no method but the one of perfection. He says: "Be whole;" "Thy faith hath made thee, whole;" "Thou art loosed from thine infirmities."

Age is not an obstacle in the way of either knowing or demonstrating the freedom of Truth. The notion that mental faculties must fail with increasing years is a false notion, and is at one with the belief that mental faculties are born of the brain, and that mind is evolved from the body. The truth is that the mental faculties, brain, and entire body are born of mind, and mind can never fails. Hence, you are always just old enough to be well, and to think right, and to know and remember all there is in truth. Now is just the right time to prove that you have health, and are happy and satisfied. Now is the time to bring eternal Life and immortality to light, and bear witness of the truth of what you are.

Because you have spent large sums of money trying to get well, do not hold that as an objection against trying this method. When it is once settled in your thought that you want to, and can, realize freedom and wholeness, the only question that should arise is: Do I want to realize it more than anything else? Be not divided in your thought between money and what may be accomplished. Let not money, time, or anything, be as an obstacle in your way. Your determination will not falter, if your purpose is one and not divided. Say: My birthright is health, wholeness, and satisfaction; do not barter it for any number of excuses. If necessary, give up every habit, every former way of thinking, talking, and acting, and conform all to Principle.

Jesus never denies the Christ within him, but says, in the hour of seeming need: "To this end was I born, and for this cause came I into the world, that I should bear witness unto the truth." Say: I am here to bear witness of the truth, as much in the hour of seeming need as at any other time, and this is my time. To this end was *I* born. My existence bears witness of truth and life. I need no medicine. I cannot serve God and Mammon. The taking of medicine will not prove that I am eternal Life and Truth. I therefore declare I am the Truth and Life, and am health. I and my Father are one, and not two; hence, I am complete in Him, and find nothing to remedy in my existence. The I Am is sufficient unto all things needful.

As you have proven that all external things are powerless to give the unwavering health and satisfaction for which you have seeking, begin your work from the plane of Being, by being in God, and you will find. If you have had no opportunity of studying Divine Science, either join a class, or find some one who can give you private instruction. Find some one who understands the Truth, and agree to unite with that one; then be as faithful to Truth as you have been in obeying the doctor's directions. Put yourself entirely in the hands of Truth, and do as the healer directs. Argue not in your thought.

Do not talk as if you were personally too good to have brought about your conditions, but that God brought them upon you, and that you must, therefore, endure. Let the Christ knowledge speak in you in all things. Say that nothing that I have believed in the past can prevent the thought of God in the demonstration of freedom for me. Do not criticize this "new and living method," Divine Science, nor condemn the statements made by the teacher and healer; for if you ask, and ask not amiss, it is necessary that you assume, mentally, the attitude of one receiving. See, therefore, that you are willing to receive, by gladly acknowledging that you do possess what you have asked for. Your teacher and healer, knowing what is the truth, will give you the necessary instruction to lead you into the consciousness of Truth.

Expect no one to devote their time to you without making some return for it. The law of giving is also the law of receiving, and the entire business of the world is transacted through this law of exchange, or law of giving and receiving, and receiving and giving. It is both spiritually and literally true that they who give, receive; and they who receive, give. Equal exchange, in the business world, is justice. The great desire of the world that is under general cultivation in the world is that of getting something for less than what it is worth. This desire prevents many from realizing wholeness; for it is just the opposite of the work of the Holy Spirit, and of divine justice, which renders exact measure according to that which is given. There is no real freedom in this desire, nor is there any real possession in the desire to get something without rendering a just equivalent. As "the laborer is worthy of his hire," one might as justly demand another's money for nothing as to demand that one should give his time and labor for nothing. To render a just equivalent for all things, in our dealings with each other, is honorable, righteous, and helpful.

No teacher or healer ever thinks of charging for the truth; hence, the charge is for the time spent in behalf of the students and patients.

If healing is not instantly realized, be reasonable, sincere, and willing to persevere. Do not say: I have given it a fair trial with a few treatments; but say to yourself: I am willing to believe that health is; hence, I am willing to say that I do not believe that I have any disease. Be as faithful in claiming that you have health, and that you are in a state of perfect harmony, as has been the false belief that claimed to be diseased and inharmonious. Be as willing to persevere with Truth as you have been willing to take medicine and to try external remedies; and you will soon prove that Divine Science is all you need to give you the full realization that God is your sufficiency. The instant there is perfect at-one-ment of your thought and real belief with the idea of God, you will realize freedom. Do not postpone being well to the future. Do not postpone for tomorrow what ought to be done today. The belief that you will receive by and by keeps putting off, and prevents you from realizing in the sweet, happy now. You cannot speak the truth of Infinite Spirit without saying: I am well now; I am free now; I am health now; I am satisfied now. You cannot say: I hope for these things some time, and speak the word of God. Thus it is clear that the Christ method is the demonstration of Principle. This is Life's "new and living way." Speak as God would speak, and your words will be Truth and Life, and your conditions, feelings, environments, and success will be shaped accordingly. Then will you be glad that you were told to say these things. The Infinite's idea is kept before you in this method.

Avoid thinking, talking, or reading of sickness, or of any kind of trouble. Do not describe symptoms or sensations to any one. When friends or members of your own family ask after your feelings and symptoms, if you describe them, it prevents you from yielding thoroughly to the treatments; for when these conditions are talked about, they are still in thought and memory; hence, they have not been given up. You can do much for yourself by avoiding everything that tends to keep in memory the conditions from which you wish to be free. To prove the Christ method, you are to be courageous, determined, and faithful, and think and act from the truth that you have being in God now. Study Divine Science, and get an understanding of divine law, and you will realize freedom, and be able to liberate others from their false claims and conditions. As Good, or God, is no respecter of persons, say to yourself: I can do all that has been done. "He that believeth shall do the things that I do," is a promise for all. Yet, of myself I can do nothing. It is God in me who is doing the works. The law to be demonstrated in the Christ method is mathematically exact. When wholeness is fully comprehended it is realized; and it is known that there is no disease in Truth. Ease, peace, and eternal rest are in the truth of at-one-ment. One is the number of unity, and not two.

Part II
INTRODUCTORY.

To Be, is in the present. To act, is in the present.

The result of action is in the present. Action and the result of action have no power over Being; neither do they attempt to have.

The true idea of a future is to be found in the eternity of the present. As the Life or Being, that now *is*, is eternal, we are now in Life or Being, what we shall ever be.

As eternity is an extension of the present, to *Be* at all is to Be what *is*, and is real now; and what is and is real now is eternal. The postponement of any possession, attainment or occurrence to the future is a prophecy; but the fulfillment of all prophecy must be in the present. Any and all action is in the present. We cannot begin the accomplishment of any work in the past or future; hence the beginning is always in the present; so, "when ye pray, believe that ye receive, and ye shall have." There can be no result in the present without acting in the present, and no present action without Being. NOW is the time to BE, to DO, and to have the example or result; for now is the accepted time. This means that the free gift of God is the perfect at-one-ment now.

It is to be understood that the treatment is to heal now; for today is the day of salvation.

These lessons are designed to correct the mistakes made by the entire race in trying to solve the problem of Life from a mental or thought standpoint, and not from the plane of Principle, or God. Hence, they strike at the root of error and all seeming discord, by whatever name called, whether sin, sickness, mental or physical, or death. They establish in thought and realization the true Christ consciousness of unity, health, harmony, and eternal life, which is the truth of I and my Father being one, and not two.

DIRECTIONS FOR APPLICATION OF

TREATMENT

God, being the infinite Whole, the one All, it is God that makes whole, or manifests in His own image and likeness. To ask in His name is to ask for or acknowledge wholeness for ourselves; and as He neither gives nor accepts anything but wholeness, to ask and ask not amiss is to offer ourselves whole and without spot or blemish, in spirit and in truth. This is keeping the covenant of at-one-ment.

In the thoughts and words of God alone is to be enjoyed the full realization of wholeness. These treatments are, therefore, intended to be used and realized a representing the truth of God speaking the absolute in all living. We can realize the true at-one-ment by virtue of our being in God and thinking His thoughts and speaking His words only. Do not hesitate to make statements that are true of God - the infinite Whole. In Truth there is nothing higher and nothing lower. Your realization of the truth of what you claim will be according to the faith that you have in your claims. To believe that you are heirs of God, and to realize that you have received and are in possession of your inheritance, is to believe that you are every whit whole, and that every part and member of your body is alive unto God forevermore.

These lessons and treatments should be committed to memory. In the application of these treatments, the student should begin with Number I (after having made the statement of Being his own) and devote one day to the study and application of each treatment, with the basic statement, by affirming its truth for all alike, and thus continue until familiar with all, and the meaning of every treatment is made fully his own and is realized to be the declaration of God within. These lessons and treatments will correct the error in belief of separation from Principle, Life, or God, just where the misconception takes place in the attempt to solve the problem of Life; and will erase the false race belief of a fall, or separation from God, and enable the student to understand and enjoy the truth that the problem of Life is already solved and demonstrated in his existence. Then will the truth of Principle be seen to spring forth speedily in health, satisfaction, and success; which may be likened to a well of pure water springing up within you unto everlasting life.

Each statement of Truth, spoken with knowledge and Faith, believing that it is true, is sufficient in itself to heal.

The numerous statements of truth have been made in the treatments, that the student may cover the ground and know that all conditions are subject to Truth and may be erased; also, that the Infinite's idea, or potentiality, may be more fully comprehended.

Before giving a treatment make the following statement: God is Infinite; and fully realize that it means He is All; and because He is All, you are: then know that all true claims are true of God, and what you claim that is true of God you are - the same has come unto you.

Go forth each day to perform your work or duties clothed with the affirmations of Truth given in the treatments, believing that you are whole and that you are not subject to conditions and influences or environments, and you will find that by thus doing the will of God the affirmations will prove to be a shield against all adverse beliefs and conditions; for against Truth there is no law. "Thy righteousness is an everlasting righteousness, and Thy law is truth." "There is no power but of God."

Basic Statements

"WHAT TO ACCEPT AND WHAT TO REJECT,
As Taught at Home College"

"STATEMENT OF BEING:

To be Understood as the Basis for Truthful
Statements, and Applied in All Treatment.

1.

There can be but one All. One is the number of unity.
Unity is to be found in the truth that the One All, is
God. God is infinite; and because there is an infinite
God, there can be nothing else.
The infinite whole is Life and all that Life contains and
manifests. Life is Love, Truth, Wisdom, Knowledge,
Substance, Intelligence, Consciousness and Power;
and all idea and goodness; and all these are principle,
and because God is all these and is All in All, a
supposition that there is separation from God, or that
there is something that is not God, is "a missing of the
mark;" falsehood; denominated sin, or the adversary;

for God says: Beside me there is none other. The Principle of wholeness is the Holy Spirit of Truth.

AT-ONE-MENT IS HARMONY.

Nothing can be made manifest that is not before it is manifested. That which *is*, can be, and is, manifested; and is an ever-present creation.

A good source cannot produce an evil result, neither can it employ any method less perfect than itself to produce that result.

ATONEMENT IS SALVATION.

"Thou shalt not partake of the knowledge of good and evil." To partake of a thing means to spiritually assimilate with, and be the thing of which we partake. To believe that there is *something* that is separated from and that is not God, is to believe that there is *something* that is separate from and is not Good; hence, to believe that there is anything that is separate from and that is not God, or Good, is to believe that there is an evil power and evil things. All conditions resulting from belief are looked upon as evil, and as being adverse to both God and Man. Error or sin, appears only a falsehood, for its beginning is in a supposition that there is separation, something that is not. Error, therefore, is no part of God or man, for they are one Truth. *Out of nothing nothing comes.* A false conception is no conception at all. It is not a living creation; it comes to nothing.

To ignore the Truth is to suspect that there is something that is not. Ignorance, therefore, is unsuspectingly taking things for what they are not.

AGREE WITH THINE ADVERSARY QUICKLY.

Falsehood is all that is the adverse of Truth; hence, falsehood is called an adversary. That which *is*, is Truth. It is impossible for anything to BE that is not. A knowledge of Truth only, can agree with, and know that the adversary is falsehood; and that a false supposition is nothing unto and is not in Truth.

TREATMENT

I.

OF AGREEMENT AND AT-ONE-MENT.

God is All, and there is nothing to resist. God is Love; there is no one to fear, none to find fault with. Non-resistance is the way of Life. I am "the way." I don't believe there is anything the adverse of Truth. Not to agree that falsehood is falsehood, is resistance; and in Truth there is nothing to resist. I agree with the adversary quickly, by agreeing that it is what it claims to be – the adverse of Truth; that error does not voice the Truth of anything that is. It represents nothing that *is*. There is no sin or separation from God in Truth. Error is nothing that is. There is no adversary in Truth. There is no condemnation in Truth.

All that *is*, is Truth. All that exists within me is Truth. I am one, perfect whole. I am agreement, unity. All that I manifest is complete within Me. Individually, my conception is *now* immaculate. The Holy Ghost has come upon me. The Spirit of wholeness is within me. My offspring is of God. My faith has made me whole. All that is manifest within me is free, *now*. My Father and I are one, and not two. I am in the enjoyment of life, liberty, and happiness. My body is the offspring of God and belongs unto Him. It has no Father or Source beside Him. Every member is a member of righteousness and power; every atom of which it is composed is alive unto God. Every atom is living unto eternity. Christ is the end of righteousness unto every one that liveth. I do now believe unto Christ-righteousness, because I know the Truth. This mind is in me which was also in Christ Jesus; who, though being in the form of God, thought it not robbery to be equal with God. There is one Spirit and one body. All that *is*, is Spirit. "That which is born of Spirit is Spirit." "My body is Spirit." Today, "a body Thou has fitted me." All things are reconciled unto God, and there is no adverse belief, condition, or disease either in God or Him manifest; either in God or creation. God and His creation are without variableness or shadow of turning. I am eternal. NOW am I unity. I now agree that sin, sickness and death, so called, are what they claim to be – non-possession; postponement; nothingness. All are now forgiven, for

I do not believe error to be anything, for the gift of God is eternal Life. Against Truth there is no law.

BASIC STATEMENT FOR TREATMENT
II.
"KNOW THE TRUTH, AND THE TRUTH SHALL MAKE YOU FREE."

To know the Truth is to perceive and know that which already *is*. To be made free by knowing the Truth is to *be* that which *is*, and is already free from all conditions that are not at one and eternal with God. What your highest conception of Divinity is, that claim to BE, and you will press forward to the mark of your high calling of at-one-ment; and "put on the whole armor of God, that ye may be able to stand": "for Christ is the end of righteousness unto every one that believeth."

TREATMENT

II.

FOR FREEDOM FROM THE FALSE CLAIMS THAT THERE IS MORTALITY.

Make the tree good and the fruit good. Affirm the following truths for all; make them fully your own; do this for the purpose of conforming all your ways to them:

God is infinite;
>Therefore, there is no finite.

Like produces like;
>Therefore, no production is the opposite of God.

God is Spirit, the only Creator;
>Therefore, there is no physical creator or creation.

That created by Spirit is Spirit;
>Therefore, no created thing is of the earth and earthly.

We are conceived in righteousness and born in true holiness;
>Therefore, we are not conceived in sin nor born in iniquity.

All forms are manifestations of Spirit;
>Therefore, there are no material forms.

We are immaculately conceived in the Spirit of wholeness, and are begotten of God;
>Therefore, we are not impurely conceived in separation nor begotten of the Flesh

In the beginning God created heaven and earth;
>Therefore, there is no material heaven or earth.

"Heaven and earth, the seas and all that in them is,"
        are living unto eternity; for God is the
        God of the living;
    Therefore, there is no heaven, or earth, or seas,
        or anything therein, that is born of time
        or place: for God is not the God of the
        dead.

The tree is good, and the fruit is good.

God is good, and I am good.

The Creator is good, and the creature is good.

God is manifest and dwelling in our midst.

God's will was done in creating earth as it was in creating heaven; and thus His law is fulfilled, against which there is no law.

BASIC STATEMENT FOR TREATMENT

III.

" I HAVE OVERCOME."

To overcome is to come over from effects unto God, who because infinite, is the only One that can produce a living thing, and thus be above all effects: then, have no beliefs the opposite of God. It is true that I am hid with Christ in God; hence, my possibility is God's possibility or idea of Himself; and my existence is this possibility or idea made manifest; for beside God there is none other. It is God who says: Be ye holy, because I am holy. As God-knowledge is all knowledge, or as God is all-knowing, we cannot have knowledge apart from Him.

Knowledge does not consist of suffering, of failure, or dissatisfaction. For this reason, from the standpoint of at-one-ment, we can wipe out the false sense of suffering, of failure and dissatisfaction. It is God, the infinite One, who says that to know self is to know all there is to know; hence, we are neither vain nor deceitful in claiming God-knowledge; for in truth, are we blessed of the Lord. True knowledge is a certain perception of the truth of at-one-ment.

TREATMENT
III.
FOR RECONCILIATION AND PERFECT
ADJUSTMENT.

"THE WORDS THAT I SPEAK, THEY ARE SPIRIT AND THEY ARE LIFE."

There is no enmity. I am infinite and all-pervading Love. I, Love, have manifested all things, and they live unto me. I am both Love and loving in all things that live and move and have being within me. I am unmoved by all that live. I move within and act upon all living things. I am love in the midst of all climates and changes of the weather. I am not affected by the wind, the storm, or the calm. I am touched by neither heat nor cold. My love, possesses all things and is master of all things. No power is given unto existing things, conditions, circumstances, or events that I do not give. "There is no power but of God." All that I manifest is spirit and is life. I now realize the perfect adjustment. Spirit, Mind or Life, is Father, Source and Cause of all form or creation. God is All, and effect is included in the All. There is one Spirit and one body. Spirit is Cause; form is effect in Spirit. Spirit is Intelligence, Substance and Power; form is the showing forth of Intelligence, Substance and Power, and can never be separated from its Source or Cause. Form is not made with hands and is eternal in the heavens.

Form is the silent utterance of eternal Life, and is the spoken word of that which is with God and is God in the beginning. My body is not subject to a false sense of things; neither is it subject to disease, or to any of the false race beliefs, that there is sin, mortality, or corruption. My body, being that which is formed, it is forever at one with the source and cause of all form. It is not the maker of itself; neither is it the maker of other forms. It is subject to nothing but God who made it. God, who made it, is its life, intelligence, substance and power. It is not sick in its life, intelligence, substance or power; and there is nothing within it the opposite of what these words imply. I am one with God, and am in no way dependent upon my body for life, intelligence, substance and power. God is His own demonstrator; His own manifester; His own revealer. I have being, demonstration, manifestation, and revelation in God only. I am the fulfillment of law and of prophecy. I have taken captivity captive. My senses are spiritual. I am self-illumined. I and my Father are one, and not two. My house is now set in order; for it is the temple of the living God, and all things therein are adjusted unto Him according to His will.

Against this there is no law.

BASIC STATEMENT FOR TREATMENT

IV.

THE WAY OF LIFE.

"Whosoever hath not, from him shall be taken even that which he thinketh that he hath."

To claim that you possess the opposite of what you are seeking, prevents the realization and enjoyment of that which is sought.

Whosoever believes that he is not whole, from him is taken away that health which he thinks he has. Health and wholeness are not realized and enjoyed.

THE BROAD WAY.

Error never claims to be life, or to be free; hence, it does not possess truth, or bear witness of anything that *is*.

Hereby know we the claims of falsehood. "Take heed how ye hear: for whosoever hath, to him shall be given."

To claim that you possess that which you have sought, gives the full realization and enjoyment of it.

Whosoever believes in his heart that he is whole, to him health is given, and wholeness is realized and enjoyed.

THE NARROW WAY.

Truth always claims to be eternal Life and to be free: hence it possesses all there is, and bears witness of what it is. Hereby know we the Spirit of Truth.

TREATMENT.

IV.

A GUIDE TO TRUTH AND TREATMENT FOR THE
REALIZATION OF PURITY OF HEART.

*"God is Spirit, and they that worship Him must
worship Him in Spirit and in Truth." "As the Father
hath life in Himself, so hath He given to the Son to
have life in Himself."*

All that *is*, is Life; for all that *is*, hath power to
be, and to bear witness of the truth, that it is eternal.
Therefore, declare in thought, word, and act, that:

There is no death, error, or ignorance within
me, For "I am" Spirit, and Spirit is Life, Truth and
Wisdom;

There is no hate, covetousness or pride of
attainment within me, For Spirit is Love, Justice, and
Perfection;

There is no doubt, fear or weakness within me,
For Spirit is Knowledge, Faith and Love;

There is no selfishness, prejudice or aversion within me, For Spirit is all-pervading presence, and has no respect to person.

There is no evil, disease, or sense of dissatisfaction within me. Spirit is Goodness, Ease, and Satisfaction;

I do not think evil thoughts. I am pure in heart and clean in thought.

I know not failure. God is His own success.

"The pure in heart see God."

"That which is born of Spirit is spirit."

"I and my Father are one, and not two."

I am free with God-freedom. I am alive with God-life. I am at rest and at one with all that is. God is my life, and my life is the life of the living. In these affirmations I worship God in the Life of the living, and in the Spirit of Truth.

I claim to have all that eternal life implies, and to *me it is given*.

BASIC STATEMENT FOR TREATMENT

V.

"STRAIT IS THE GATE AND NARROW THE WAY WHICH LEADETH UNTO LIFE; AND FEW THERE BE THAT FIND IT."

I have found that the narrow way which leads unto Life is Unity, which is the "new and living way." The way is unity. They who find it are they who see that the "outer is as the inner;" the creature as the Creator; the tree is good and the fruit is good; the All as one Infinite God manifest. I realize eternal Life and enjoy the heaven within me, because in this at-one-ment God's will is done.

To believe that evil, sin, sickness, and death are in Truth, and that we are subject to them, is to have other gods before Me. What we believe we are subject to, our beliefs are servants of. "Ye believe in God, believe also in me." This is the work of God, that ye believe on Him whom God hath sent.

TREATMENT

V.

I HAVE ENTERED IN,

THEREFORE I AFFIRM:

There is no evil power or thing. All power is of God, and all things are good.

There is no matter. All that *is*, is Spirit.

My body is not subject to pain or disease. My body lives unto God and is subject only to His peace and rest.

Feeling is not of the body. Feeling is in thought. My thoughts are the thoughts of God.

I do not sense pain. The divine Mind, which is in Christ Jesus, is the only mind.

There is no sickness in Truth. All that *is*, is free with the freedom of truth.

There is no death in Life. Life is, and is eternal; All in All.

After creation God says, "I Am that I Am, and beside Me there is none other."

"I Am, is my name forever." In at-one-ment I am to be found, and I am perfect harmony. All my works are done in truth, and perfect harmony pervades and sustains them all. Now am I the Truth that I perceive and know. Individually He is our peace, who hath made both one, and hath broken down the middle wall of partition, having abolished in his flesh the enmity. I am immersed within the infinite Good; "buried with Christ in baptism, wherein I am risen with him." I have entered in at the strait gate, and the peace of God rules in my heart. " Against me there is no law.

BASIC STATEMENT FOR TREATMENT

VI.

"HE THAT BELIEVETH ON ME,

THE WORKS THAT I DO SHALL HE DO ALSO."

To believe on Jesus, the Christ, is to know that you are in the kingdom of God's dear Son, and that you are just the same in being and existence as is Jesus, the Christ. "And at that day ye shall know that I am in the Father, and ye in Me, and I in you." The Comforter that the Father sends, which shall abide with you, is the Spirit of Truth. Now is always the time to believe in the truth of what you are; and be comforted.

TREATMENT

VI.

COMFORTING WORDS OF LIFE AND POWER.
NOW IS THE ACCEPTED TIME.

I believe that Jesus Christ is come in the flesh, and that I shall do the work of Christ. "There is, therefore, now, no condemnation to them which are in Christ Jesus." Therefore, know: I am the Light that is come into the world, and say:

There is no fear;

For God is all-pervading Love.

There can be no fear of separation from God within me;

For God is One and inseparable.

There can be no fear of sin, sickness, or sorrow within me;

For now am I saved, my health is established, and my joy is complete.

There can be no fear of death, weakness, or want within me;

47

For God is my Life, strength, and supply.
There is no fear, anxious care or doubt within me;
For I dwell in Love, and Love dwells in
me.
There is no fear that I shall become helpless and
burdensome to my friends.
For the gift of God is Eternal Life, and I
am this life, ever active and free from burden.
I do not fear age of body;
For my body is living unto eternity.
There can be no failure of mental faculties, sight, or
hearing;
For in God there is no failure. He is my
unfailing sight and hearing.
God hath not given us the spirit of fear;
For He has given us the spirit of power,
and of Love,
and of a sound mind.

I, Love, resist not, fear not, doubt not. Because
Love is without fear, it knows not fear. I am complete
and perfect in God-love. I am Life, Intelligence, and
Power. I now realize that I possess all for which I have

asked. I am in the Holy of Holies; self-illumined. I demonstrate perfect health, peace and satisfaction. I am at rest in my thoughts. I am clean in thought and pure in heart. I see God as All in All, and I have no life or selfhood apart from Him. I am satisfied and happy. I am lifted up from the earth and have drawn all unto me.

"Now is the accepted time;" now is God's law fulfilled. I have entered into his rest.

M. E. Cramer

BASIC STATEMENT FOR TREATMENT

VII.

"ALL THINE ARE MINE AND ALL MINE ARE
THINE."

Our inheritance is purity throughout, mentally
and visibly. We are heirs of God and joint heirs with
Christ. In Christ, the creature itself has the glorious
liberty of a child of God, and is heir of God. The spirit
of wholeness and power thus declares it, and that in
substance it is free from the beliefs of corruption and
mortality.

When anything is bequeathed to us, there is a
specified time when we are to receive it. *Now* is the
accepted time, specified by Eternity to *Be*, and possess.
To-day is *the day* of salvation; hence it is to be
understood that there is no mortality within Life.
"Thanks be to God who giveth us the victory through
our Lord Jesus Christ," of the redemption of our body.
Since this is the Truth is that God is the One All and
yet I am, there is no true idea of possession that is not
conveyed in the words of Christ. "All Mine are Thine,

and all Thine are Mine, and I am glorified in them;" hence, "If I judge, My judgment is truth."

TREATMENT

VII.

"ALL POWER IN HEAVEN AND IN EARTH IS GIVEN UNTO ME."

THE HOLY SPIRIT IS HERE AND I AM HERE.

Because the Holy Spirit is, I am holy. Now I am in possession of my inheritance bequeathed by the Father. Now I possess all possibility that I can ever manifest. I am *eternal* Life, and I manifest it fully. I am in the Spirit, and it is the Lord's day. I have been baptized unto Christ and have put on Christ. He who anoints with the Spirit of Truth is God. I am perfect in thought and word, motive and deed. I am harmonious in feeling and sensation. I am accurate and definite in all that I think and do. I am the true idea of success; and failure I know not, for failure is not. I am sight, hearing, faith, power, and understanding. I manifest love, charity, harmony, and peace. The divine attributes are manifest in all that I think and do. I am not a servant, but a son, radiating the light and glorifying the life of the Infinite One. I am steadfast in the liberty with which eternal Life is free. My possessions are immortal, incorruptible, unalterable. The whole earth and the fullness thereof is lifted up unto me. Father, in this I have glorified Thee on earth; I ihave finishesd the work which Thou hast given me to do. All mine are Thine and all Thine are mine. Of all that Thou hast given me I can lose nothing; for of all that are Thine, nothing can be lost. All Thine are at one with Thee, and all Thine are at one with me, and I am glorified in them. I have received my inheritance. I have accepted the truth that there is no corruption, and no mortality, and death is swallowed up of Life, and that there is no enemy. God is Life, and beside Him there is no Life.

"Be still and Know That I Am God."

Against these affirmations of wholeness and at-one-ment, there is no law.

SPECIFIC TREATMENT
VIII.
AGAINST THE BELIEF IN LIMITATION, AND THE DESIRE FOR LIQUOR.

In this manner prepare and make receptive your thought to apply the following treatment:

Our Father, which art Infinite and everywhere present, we turn to Thee for every blessing. We thank Thee for the knowledge that Thou art All, and art in all, - the ever-present Life and living good. As such, we glorify Thee in the spirit of wholeness, and worship Thee "on earth." We sanctify in Thy Truth all things made, because Thou sanctifiest all with thy presence - Thy eternal Being. We love to say there is no limitation to or lack of goodness in the vast universe of Cause and effect; for in acknowledging this Truth we entertain Thee as our constant companion and enjoy Thy presence without omission. We love to affirm the Truth for all, that Thou hast made all things like unto Thyself, and placed upon them no limitation; for truly Thou dost not measure thy spirit to Thy children. Thy wholeness of Being is given unto each and all alike.

We love to say that now is our brother in Thy Being, the all-embracing love and sustaining power.

Thou art the only Being to sustain and guide his thought aright in paths of peace. We understand that Thou hast made him whole, pure and good, and that there is nothing impure or unholy in and of itself; and as Thou hast pronounced all things good, forbid that we pronounce against Thee.

TREATMENT

VIII.

There is no attribute or idea of limitation in God, sensuous appetite and desire; hence, our brother is not the seeming appetite or desire for liquor, which sensuous beliefs claim him to be. He cannot express anything real that does not represent the divine attributes of Being; therefore, he is free in Truth at this time; nothing binds or limits him.

Thou art, O God, pronouncing him good, free and whole, in Thy limitless Being and Love at this time.

Dear brother James, listen to the voice of the Spirit of God speaking within you, "You do not slumber in sense delusion; there is no sense delusion. You are not limited or controlled by desire. There is no desire in Truth. You are free to hear and understand My supreme words of freedom. This voice says you are free to witness My presence working in you. Listen, and understand what I say to you: liquor is neither the life, intelligence, substance, power, nor peace for which you are seeking. It cannot give you strength, success, health, or satisfaction; it is effect and can never be a cause and source of happiness to you. You do not believe that you desire or need it; you know that you are immortal and have eternal life with Me. You are in no way dependent upon liquor for either health, strength, success, or happiness. I, alone, am the source of all that you need. Your body is radiant with My presence now. The Truth that I speak unto you has erased all false belief, and darkness has disappeared. You now understand that what I say to you is Truth. I am your Life, your love, your truth, your substance, your peace, and you are filled with perfect satisfaction at this time.

My brother and I thank Thee, O Infinite Source of all Good, that we know that Thou art throughout the vast universe; and that we are all resting within Thee, and that Thou art our abiding place now and forever. Amen!

"Behold! thou art made whole."

M. E. Cramer

Wisewoman Press
Vancouver, WA 98665
800.603.3005
www.wisewomanpress.com

Books Published by WiseWoman Press

By Emma Curtis Hopkins

- *Resume*
- *The Gospel Series*
- *Class Lessons of 1888*
- *Self Treatments including Radiant I Am*
- *High Mysticism*
- *Genesis Series 1894*
- *Esoteric Philosophy in Spiritual Science*
- *Drops of Gold Journal*
- *Judgment Series*
- *Bible Interpretations: Series I, thru XVII*

By Ruth L. Miller

- *Unveiling Your Hidden Power: Emma Curtis Hopkins'*
  Metaphysics for the 21st Century
- *Coming into Freedom: Emily Cady's Lessons in Truth for the*
  21st Century
- *150 Years of Healing: The Founders and Science of New*
  Thought
- *Power Beyond Magic: Ernest Holmes Biography*
- *Power to Heal: Emma Curtis Hopkins Biography*
- *The Power of Unity: Charles Fillmore Biography*
- *Power of Thought: Phineas P. Quimby Biography*
- *The Power of Insight: Thomas Troward Biography*
- *The Power of Mind: Ralph Waldo Emerson Biography*
- *Gracie's Adventures with God*
- *Uncommon Prayer*
- *Spiritual Success*
- *Finding the Path*

Books Published by WiseWoman Press
By Malinda Cramer

- *Basic Statements and Health Treatment of Truth*
- *Lessons in the Science of Infinite Spirit and Christ method of Healing (Kindle and ebook only)*

By Ute Maria Cedilla

- *The Mysticism of Emma Curtis Hopkins Volume 1 Realizing the Christ Within*
- *The Mysticism of Emma Curtis Hopkins Volume 2 Ministry: Realizing The Christ One In All*

By Frances B. Lancaster

- *Abundance Now*
- *Happiness Now*
- *The 13th Commandment*
- *A Miracle of Love*

By Christine Green

- *Authentic Spirituality – A Woman's Guide to Living a Spiritually Empowered Life*
- *Anatomy of Caring*
- *A Caregivers Journal*

By Cath DePalma

- *I Can Do This Thing Called Life: and So Can You*

By Kathianne Lewis

- *40 Days to Freedom – with Emma Curtis Hopkins*
- *40 Days to Power – with excerpts of the work of Emma Curtis Hopkins*

Most books are Available as ebooks and Kindle

from Amazon and www.wisewomanpress.com

M. E. Cramer

www.ingramcontent.com/pod-product-compliance
Lightning Source LLC
Chambersburg PA
CBHW072013060426
42446CB00043B/2431